FAVORITE *Disney* FOR PIANO DUET

ISBN 978-1-5400-3874-6

DISTRIBUTED BY

Visit Hal Leonard Online at
www.halleonard.com

Contact us:
Hal Leonard
7777 West Bluemound Road
Milwaukee, WI 53213
Email: info@halleonard.com

In Europe, contact:
Hal Leonard Europe Limited
42 Wigmore Street
Marylebone, London, W1U 2RN
Email: info@halleonardeurope.com

In Australia, contact:
Hal Leonard Australia Pty. Ltd.
4 Lentara Court
Cheltenham, Victoria, 3192 Australia
Email: info@halleonard.com.au

CAN YOU FEEL THE LOVE TONIGHT

from THE LION KING

SECONDO

Music by ELTON JOHN
Lyrics by TIM RICE

Slowly and expressively

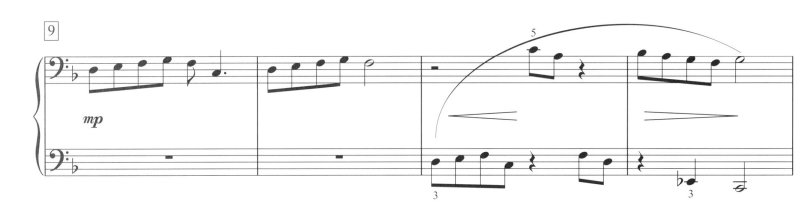

CAN YOU FEEL THE LOVE TONIGHT

from THE LION KING

PRIMO

Music by ELTON JOHN
Lyrics by TIM RICE

6

SECONDO

PRIMO

DO YOU WANT TO BUILD A SNOWMAN?

from FROZEN

SECONDO

Music and Lyrics by KRISTEN ANDERSON-LOPEZ
and ROBERT LOPEZ

Moderate, rhythmic

DO YOU WANT TO BUILD A SNOWMAN?

from FROZEN

PRIMO

Music and Lyrics by KRISTEN ANDERSON-LOPEZ
and ROBERT LOPEZ

SECONDO

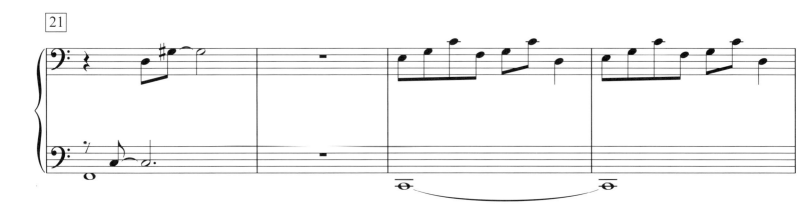

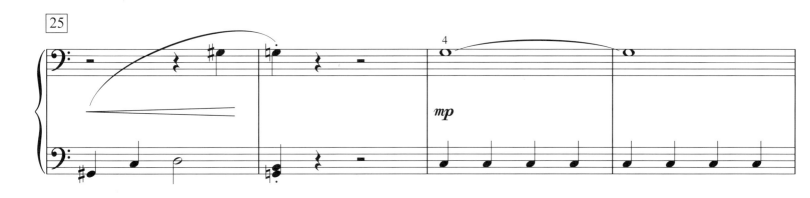

PRIMO

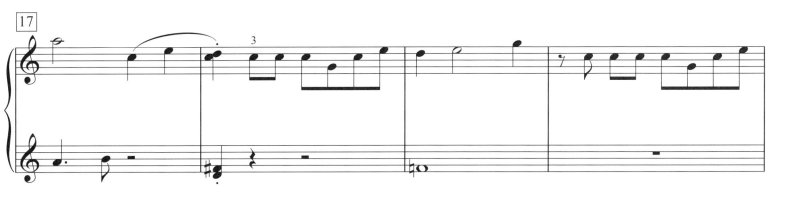

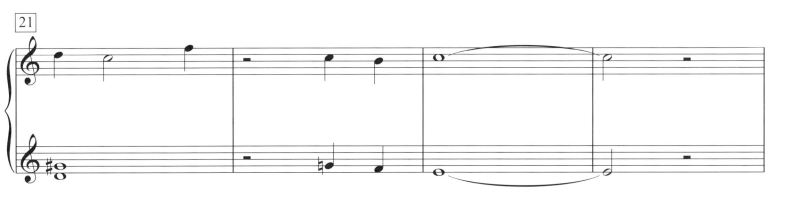

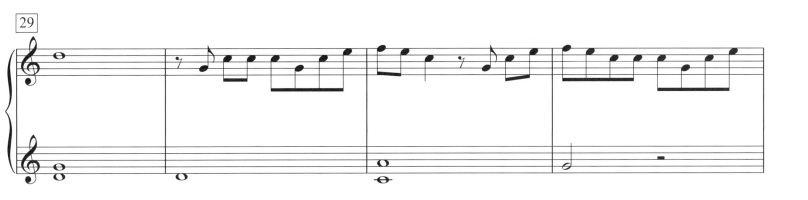

SECONDO

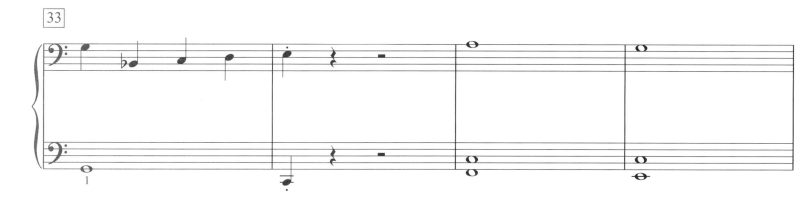

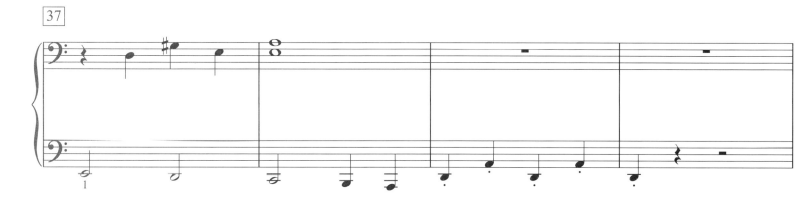

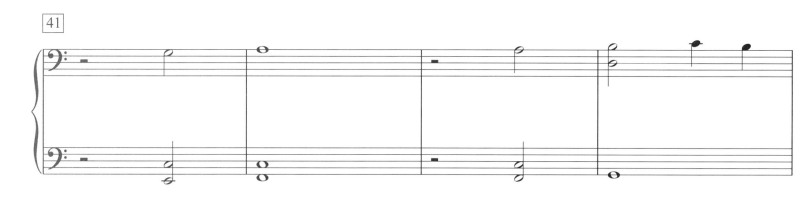

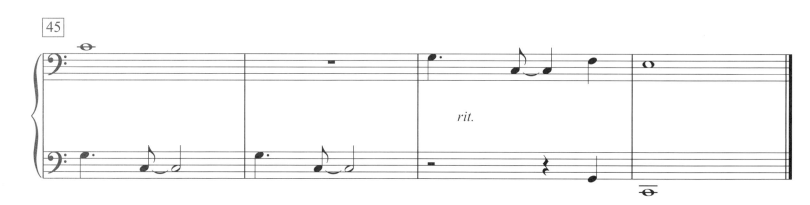

PRIMO

A DREAM IS A WISH YOUR HEART MAKES

from CINDERELLA

SECONDO

Music by MACK DAVID and AL HOFFMAN
Lyrics by JERRY LIVINGSTON

Slowly and gently

A DREAM IS A WISH YOUR HEART MAKES

from CINDERELLA

PRIMO

Music by MACK DAVID and AL HOFFMAN
Lyrics by JERRY LIVINGSTON

SUPERCALIFRAGILISTICEXPIALIDOCIOUS

from MARY POPPINS

SECONDO

Words and Music by RICHARD M. SHERMAN
and ROBERT B. SHERMAN

SUPERCALIFRAGILISTICEXPIALIDOCIOUS
from MARY POPPINS

PRIMO

Words and Music by RICHARD M. SHERMAN
and ROBERT B. SHERMAN

18

SECONDO

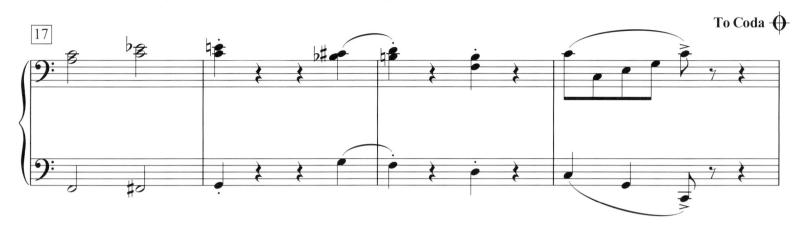

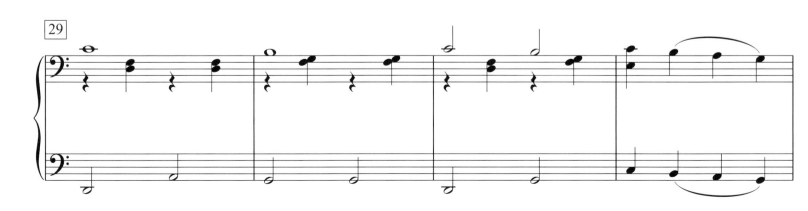

PRIMO

To Coda ⊕

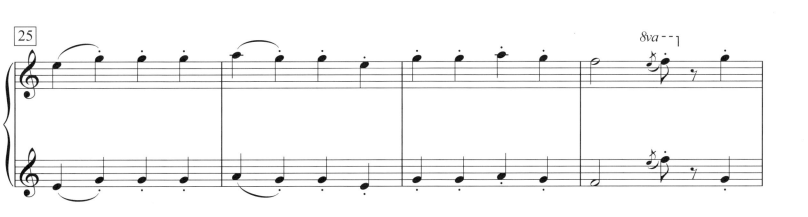

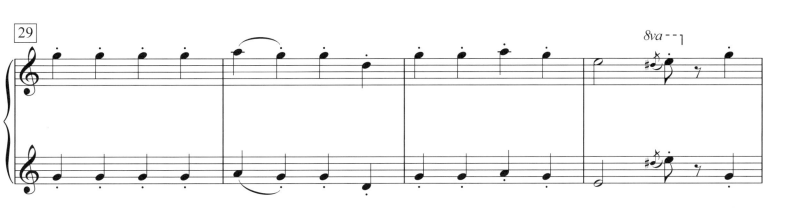

SECONDO

D.S. al Coda

CODA

p *gradual cresc. to end*

ff

PRIMO

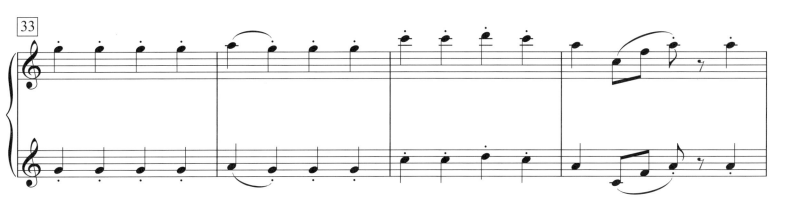

D.S. al Coda

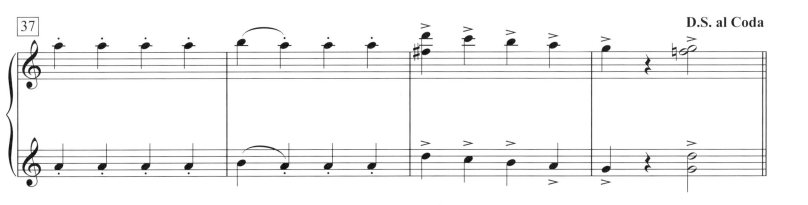

CODA

THAT'S HOW YOU KNOW
from ENCHANTED

SECONDO

Music by ALAN MENKEN
Lyrics by STEPHEN SCHWARTZ

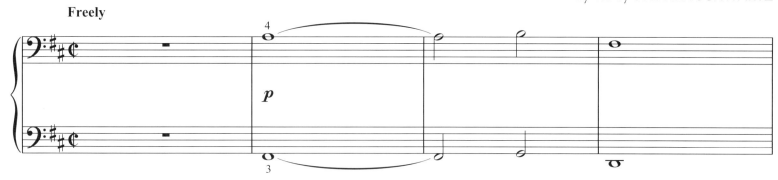

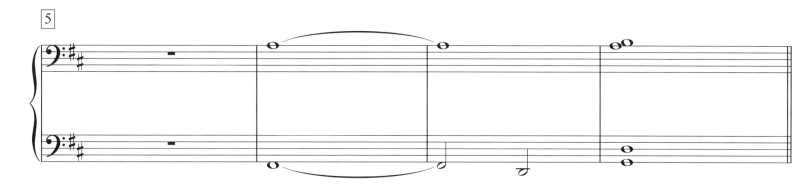

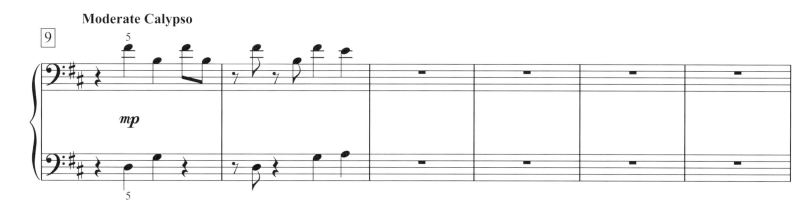

THAT'S HOW YOU KNOW
from ENCHANTED

PRIMO

Music by ALAN MENKEN
Lyrics by STEPHEN SCHWARTZ

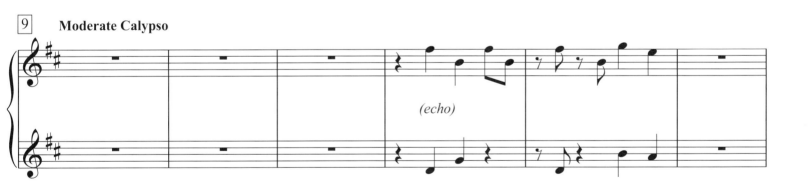

SECONDO

PRIMO

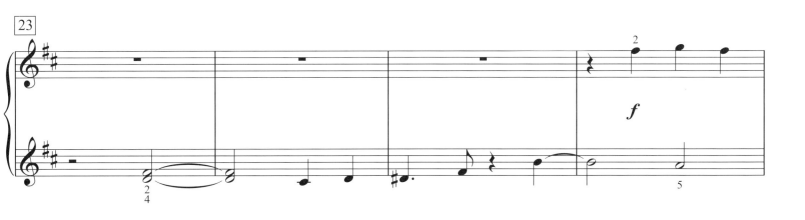

SECONDO

PRIMO

WHEN WILL MY LIFE BEGIN?
from TANGLED

SECONDO

Music by ALAN MENKEN
Lyrics by GLENN SLATER

WHEN WILL MY LIFE BEGIN?

from TANGLED

PRIMO

Music by ALAN MENKEN
Lyrics by GLENN SLATER

SECONDO

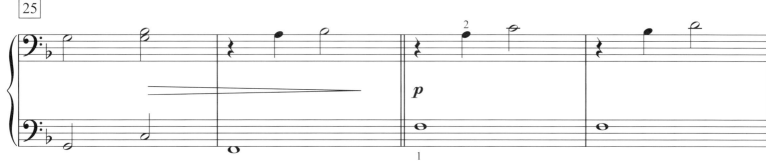

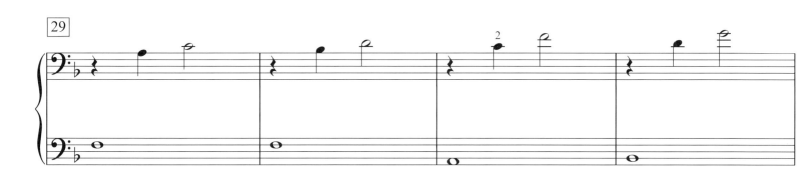

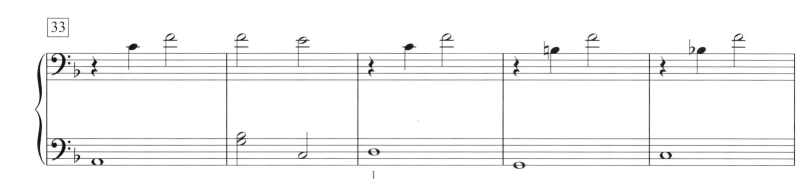

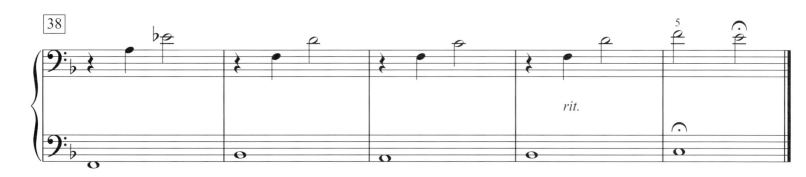

PRIMO

YOU'LL BE IN MY HEART

(Pop Version)
from TARZAN®

SECONDO

Words and Music by
PHIL COLLINS

Moderately

(Knuckle on wood)

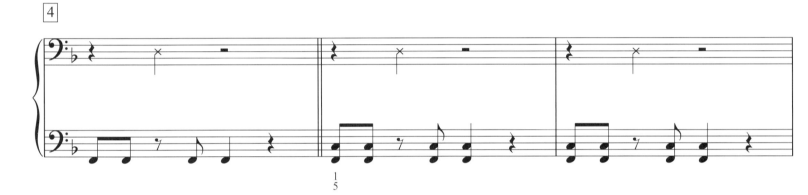

YOU'LL BE IN MY HEART
(Pop Version)
from TARZAN®

PRIMO

Words and Music by
PHIL COLLINS

SECONDO

SECONDO

PRIMO

YOU'VE GOT A FRIEND IN ME

from TOY STORY

SECONDO

Music and Lyrics by
RANDY NEWMAN

YOU'VE GOT A FRIEND IN ME
from TOY STORY

PRIMO

Music and Lyrics by
RANDY NEWMAN

Easy Shuffle

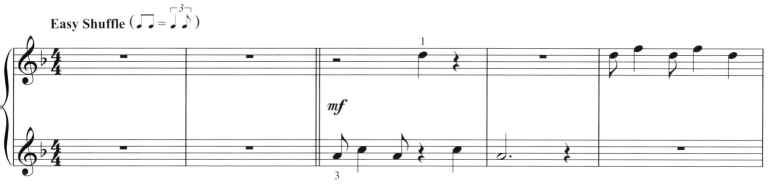

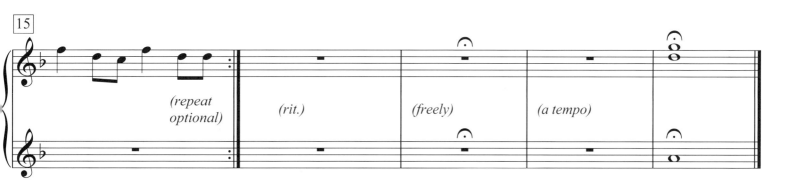

Play Your Favorite Disney Songs

Piano/Vocal/Guitar

00312480	Aladdin	$17.99
00359047	Alice in Wonderland	$16.99
00313000	And the Winner Is – 2nd Ed.	$17.99
00313055	The Aristocats	$14.99
00234049	Beauty and the Beast (2017)	$19.99
00311532	Beauty and the Beast Selections from the Movie	$17.99
00359192	The Best of Disney	$14.99
00103145	Brave	$16.99
00313499	Camp Rock 2 – The Final Jam	$16.99
00242528	Cars 3	$14.99
00359478	Cinderella	$14.99
00146069	Cinderella (2015)	$16.99
00253985	Coco	$17.99
00195620	Contemporary Disney – 3rd Edition	$22.99
00151969	Descendants	$17.99
00237613	Descendants 2	$17.99
00311523	The Disney Collection	$22.50
00283395	Disney Love Songs - 3rd Edition	$16.99
00313205	The Disney Theme Park Songbook	$19.99
00313588	Disney's Fairy Tale Weddings	$16.99
00313123	Disney's Greatest Pop Hits	$16.99
00313184	Disney's Princess Collection – Complete	$19.99
00248638	Disney Villains	$16.99
00313393	Enchanted	$16.99
00124307	Frozen	$17.99
00313073	Hercules	$19.99
00313329	High School Musical	$24.99
00313045	The Hunchback of Notre Dame	$19.99
00256650	The Illustrated Treasury of Disney Songs – 7th Ed.	$32.99
00360154	Walt Disney's The Jungle Book	$16.99
00313109	Lady and the Tramp	$10.95
00156370	The Lion Guard	$16.99
00312504	The Lion King	$17.99
00313624	The Lion King – Deluxe Edition	$19.99
00490238	The Little Mermaid	$17.99
00360439	Mary Poppins	$15.99
00204662	Moana	$17.99
00313099	Mulan	$16.99
00127534	The Muppets Most Wanted	$16.99
00311572	Newsies	$17.99
00315560	Newsies – Broadway Musical	$19.99
00253989	Olaf's Frozen Adventure	$16.99
00360819	Peter Pan	$14.99
00313013	Pocahontas	$19.99
00313482	The Princess and the Frog	$16.99
00125526	Saving Mr. Banks	$14.99
00311525	A Souvenir Disney Songbook	$24.99
00313524	Tangled	$16.99
00313122	Tarzan	$17.99
00122118	Teen Beach Movie	$16.99
00313033	Toy Story	$12.99

Easy Piano

00222555	Aladdin	$12.99
00130670	Aladdin – Broadway Musical	$19.99
00110003	Beauty and the Beast	$16.95
00234050	Beauty and the Beast (2017)	$17.99
00316039	Disney's Beauty and the Beast: The Broadway Musical	$17.99
00248749	Cars	$12.99
00285558	Christopher Robin	$17.99
00146948	Cinderella (2015)	$14.99
00254119	Coco	$17.99
00316040	Disney!	$19.99
00222535	The Disney Collection	$19.99
00119716	The Disney Collection	$27.50
00193589	Disney Fun Songs	$14.99
00192459	Disney Greatest Love Songs	$14.99
00316075	Disney Hits	$12.99
00286966	Disney Latest Hits	$14.99
00316081	Disney Mega-Hit Movies – 2nd Ed.	$19.99
00310322	Disney's My First Songbook	$16.99
00316085	Disney's My First Songbook – Vol. 2	$14.95
00316123	Disney's My First Songbook – Vol. 3	$14.99
00316160	Disney's My First Songbook – Vol. 4	$17.99
00140978	Disney's My First Songbook – Vol. 5	$14.99
00313057	Disney's Princess Collection – Vol. 1	$14.99
00316034	Disney's Princess Collection – Vol. 2	$14.99
00316121	Enchanted	$12.95
00490553	Fantasia	$14.99
00194350	Finding Dory	$14.99
00274938	First 50 Disney Songs You Should Play on the Piano	$16.99
00125506	Frozen	$17.99
00279514	Frozen – The Broadway Musical	$19.99
00142790	Into the Woods	$16.99
00254118	Olaf's Frozen Adventure	$14.99
00316047	Walt Disney's The Jungle Book	$12.99
00316122	The Lion King – Broadway Selections	$17.99
00110029	The Lion King	$17.99
00490386	The Little Mermaid	$15.95
00316018	Mary Poppins	$12.99
00204664	Moana	$16.99
00119440	Newsies – Broadway Musical	$16.99
00316096	Pirates of the Caribbean – The Curse of the Black Pearl	$16.99
00311916	Really Easy Piano – Disney	$14.99
00316153	Toy Story Easy Piano Collection	$14.99
00129727	Up	$14.99
00277257	A Wrinkle in Time	$17.99
00276975	Zombies	$17.99

Piano Solo

00313495	Alice in Wonderland	$17.99
00242909	Beauty and the Beast (2017)	$16.99
00192070	The BFG	$17.99
00285000	Christopher Robin	$17.99
00313131	Disney at the Piano	$15.99
00313150	Disney Classics	$12.95
00128219	Disney Hits for Piano Solo	$16.99
00242588	Disney Medleys for Piano Solo	$16.99
00313128	Disney Piano Solos	$14.99
00313527	Disney Songs	$14.99
00311754	Disney Songs for Classical Piano	$16.99
00292006	Fantasia	$15.99
00194289	Finding Dory	$16.99
00128220	Frozen	$14.99
00154672	The Good Dinosaur	$16.99
00313290	The Incredibles	$14.95
00282473	Incredibles 2	$17.99
00148723	Inside Out	$14.99
00292060	The Lion King	$12.95
00131318	Maleficent	$14.99
00122213	The Monsters Collection	$16.99
00242537	Pirates of the Caribbean – Dead Men Tell No Tales	$16.99
00313579	Pirates of the Caribbean – On Stranger Tides	$16.99
00313380	Pirates of the Caribbean – At World's End	$16.99
00313343	Pirates of the Caribbean – Dead Man's Chest	$16.99
00313256	Pirates of the Caribbean – The Curse of the Black Pearl	$19.99
00148720	Tomorrowland	$14.99
00313471	Up	$16.99

Piano/Vocal

00126656	Aladdin – Broadway Musical	$19.99
00312511	Disney's Beauty and the Beast: The Broadway Musical	$22.99
00230066	Disney Collected Kids' Solos	$34.99
00740197	Disney Solos for Kids	$19.99
00281007	Frozen – The Broadway Musical	$19.99
00313097	The Lion King – Broadway Selections	$19.99
00313402	The Little Mermaid	$22.99
00313303	Mary Poppins	$17.99
00740294	More Disney Solos for Kids	$19.99
00230032	Still More Disney Solos for Kids	$19.99

Fake Books

00175311	The Disney Fake Book – 4th Edition	$30.00

HAL•LEONARD®

Disney Characters and Artwork TM & © 2018 Disney

Prices, contents, and availability subject to change without notice.
Prices listed in U.S. dollars.